STRIKING DISTANCE

Harry Gamboa Jr.

STRIKING DISTANCE

©2020, Harry Gamboa Jr.
All Rights Reserved
ISBN: 9798669765798
Imprint: Independently published

In memory of familiar faces

Notes - July 2020

The secret police are brutally beating Navy veterans who are risking their lives in defense of the U.S. Constitution. Mothers have organized themselves to stand between violent batons, rubber bullets, chemical sprays and gases, in order to protect young protesters from being kidnapped and maimed. The unidentified militarized storm troopers attack with impunity. Journalists are blinded and jailed. Fascism and Martial Law threatens to take a chockhold against democracy.

Police murder **George Perry Floyd Jr.**, sparking an illuminated **BLM** consciousness of antiracism across the world causing symbolic actions with statues being defaced, removed, or publicly tumbled (Confederate Generals, King Leopold II, Junipero Serra, Cecil Rhodes, Christopher Columbus, Louis XVI, Jefferson Davis, Chief Justice Roger Taney). Trump's Border Wall will collapse as a fragile façade of false superiority.

Brilliant artists, **Cassils** and **rafa esparza**, envision **In Plain Sight** to actualize nationwide support for Immigrant Rights by enlisting many artists and an expert fleet of small planes to skytype words and phrases that appeared over major cities and other areas where ICE engages private detention centers to violate Human Rights by placing children in cages, separating families, and holding people in dangerous confined areas. For a moment, my contribution was emblazoned across the sky above Mesa Verde Detention Center in Bakersfield. The captive immigrants chanted the words, **NO ICE, NO ICE, NO ICE**, in defiance of the mercinary guards and within earshot of pro-immigrant supporters who were protesting at the gated entry of the infamous site.

California has the most COVID-19 cases in U.S. as it rages illness and death making Los Angeles an ultimate viral hot spot.

STRIKING DISTANCE, portraits in pandemic, featuring many of my favorite Los Angeles-based artists, writers, thinkers, and makers. COVID-19 vs. Leica D-Lux 7.

Thanks and Appreciation:
Autry Museum of the American West, Williams College Museum of Art, and **Museum Ludwig**.

Harry Gamboa Jr.
Striking Distance #1

16 inches x 20 inches
FujiFlex Lightjet Print
Edition of three

Performer: Suné Woods

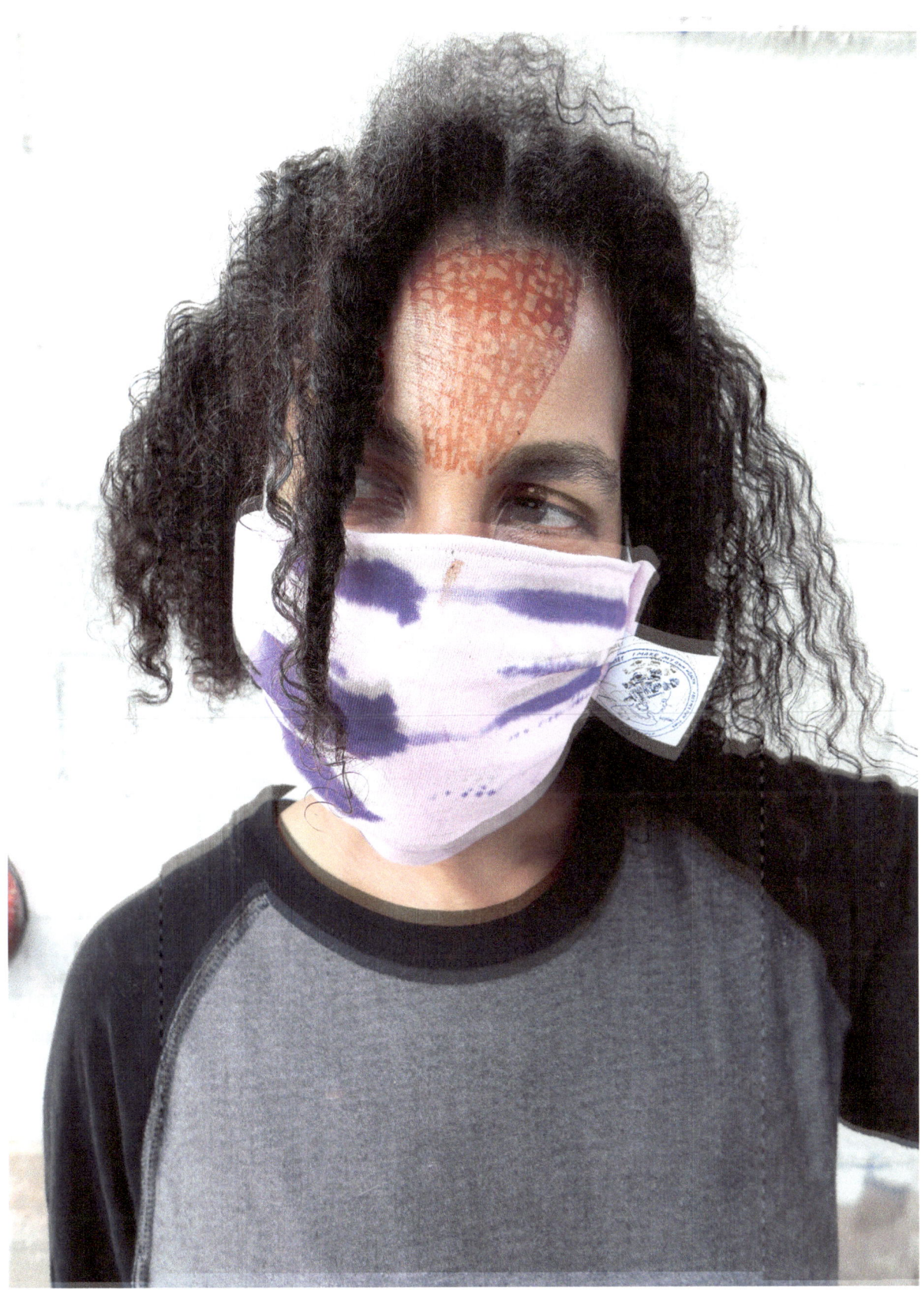

Harry Gamboa Jr.
Striking Distance #2

16 inches x 20 inches
FujiFlex Lightjet Print
Edition of three

Performer: Benjamin Quiñones

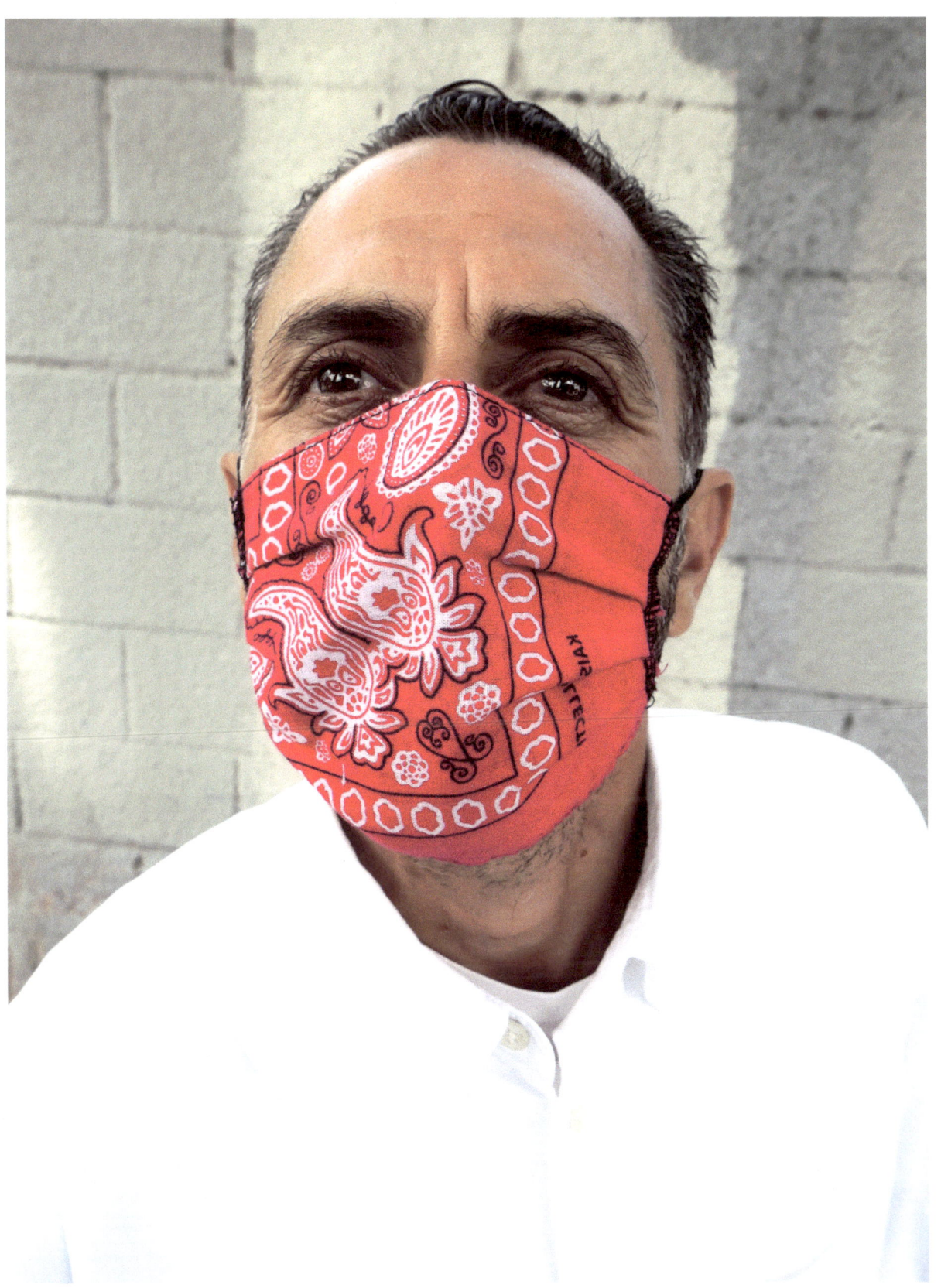

Harry Gamboa Jr.
Striking Distance #3

16 inches x 20 inches
FujiFlex Lightjet Print
Edition of three

Performer: Francesco X. Siqueiros

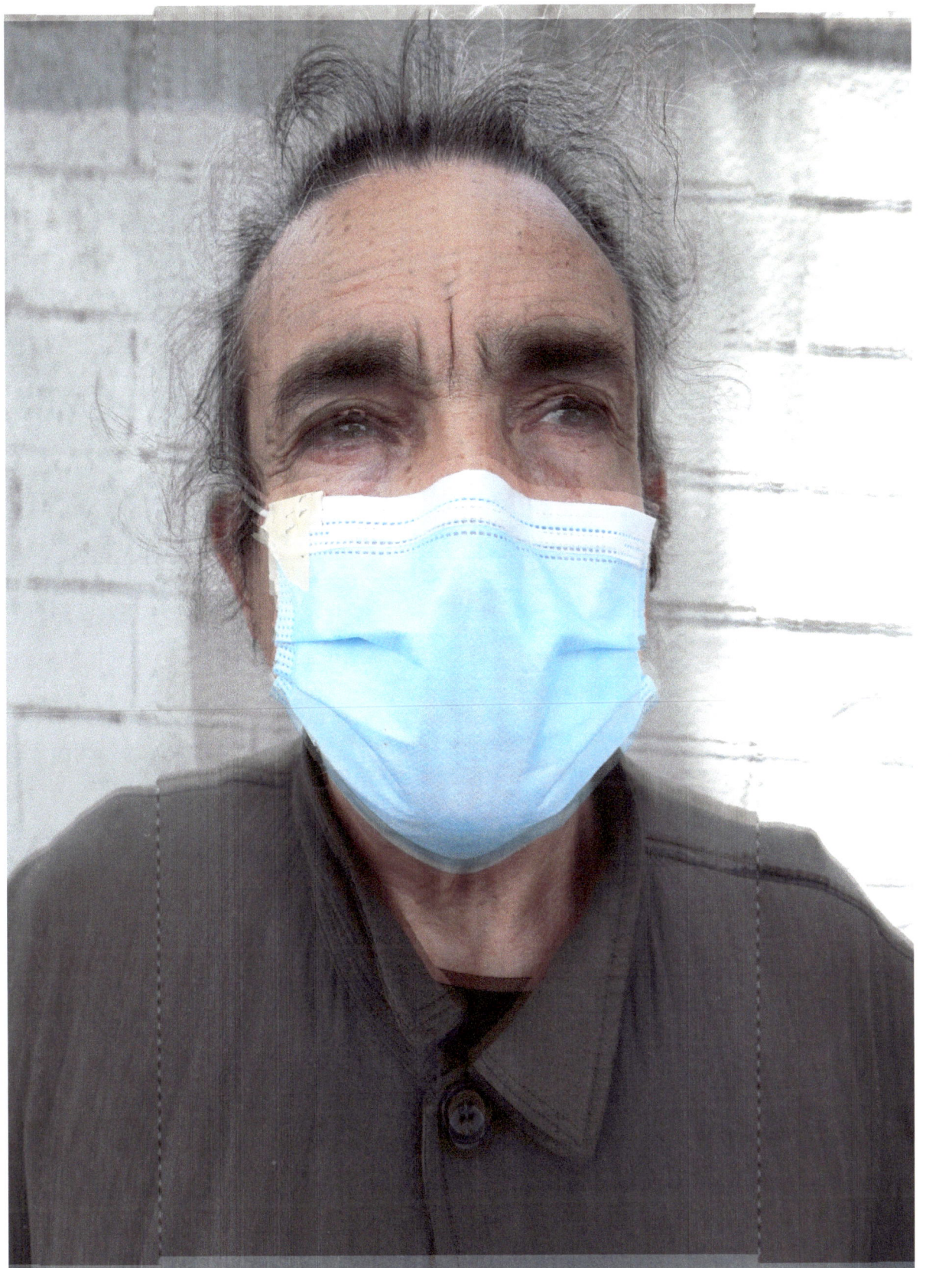

Harry Gamboa Jr.
Striking Distance #4

16 inches x 20 inches
FujiFlex Lightjet Print
Edition of three

Performer: Calvin Lee

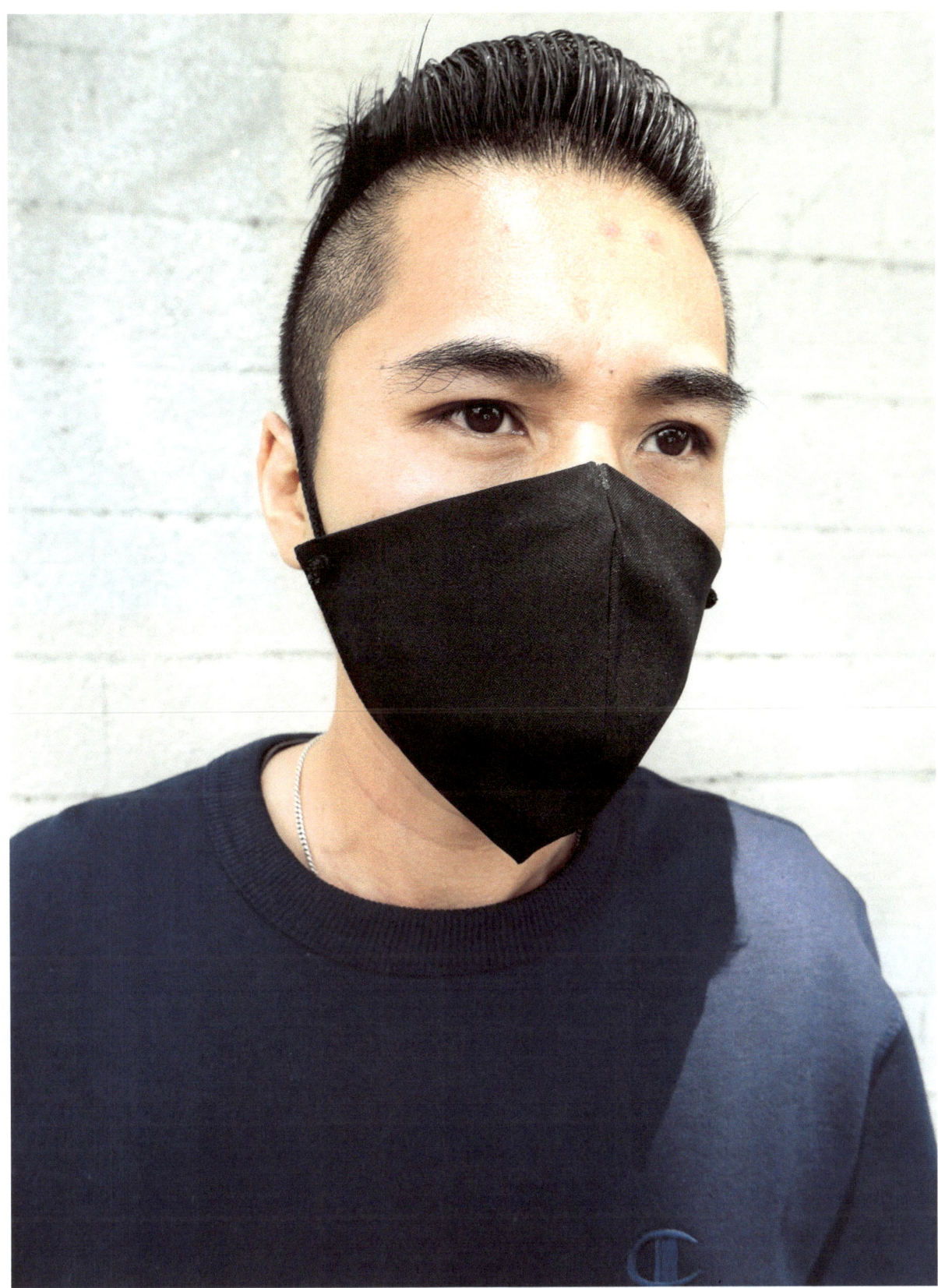

Harry Gamboa Jr.
Striking Distance #5

16 inches x 20 inches
FujiFlex Lightjet Print
Edition of three

Performer: Jazmin Urrea

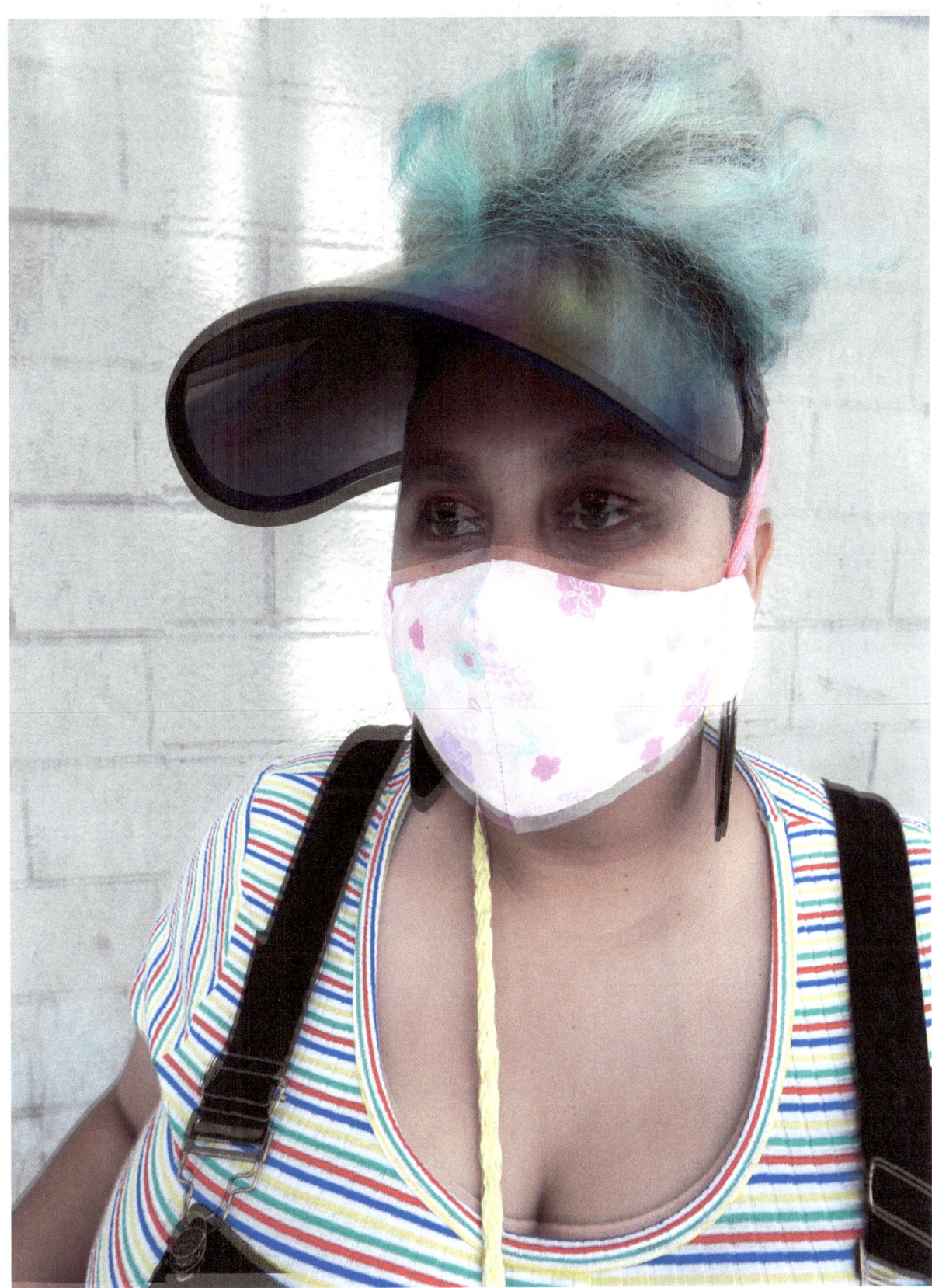

Harry Gamboa Jr.
Striking Distance #6

16 inches x 20 inches
FujiFlex Lightjet Print
Edition of three

Performer: Henry Williams

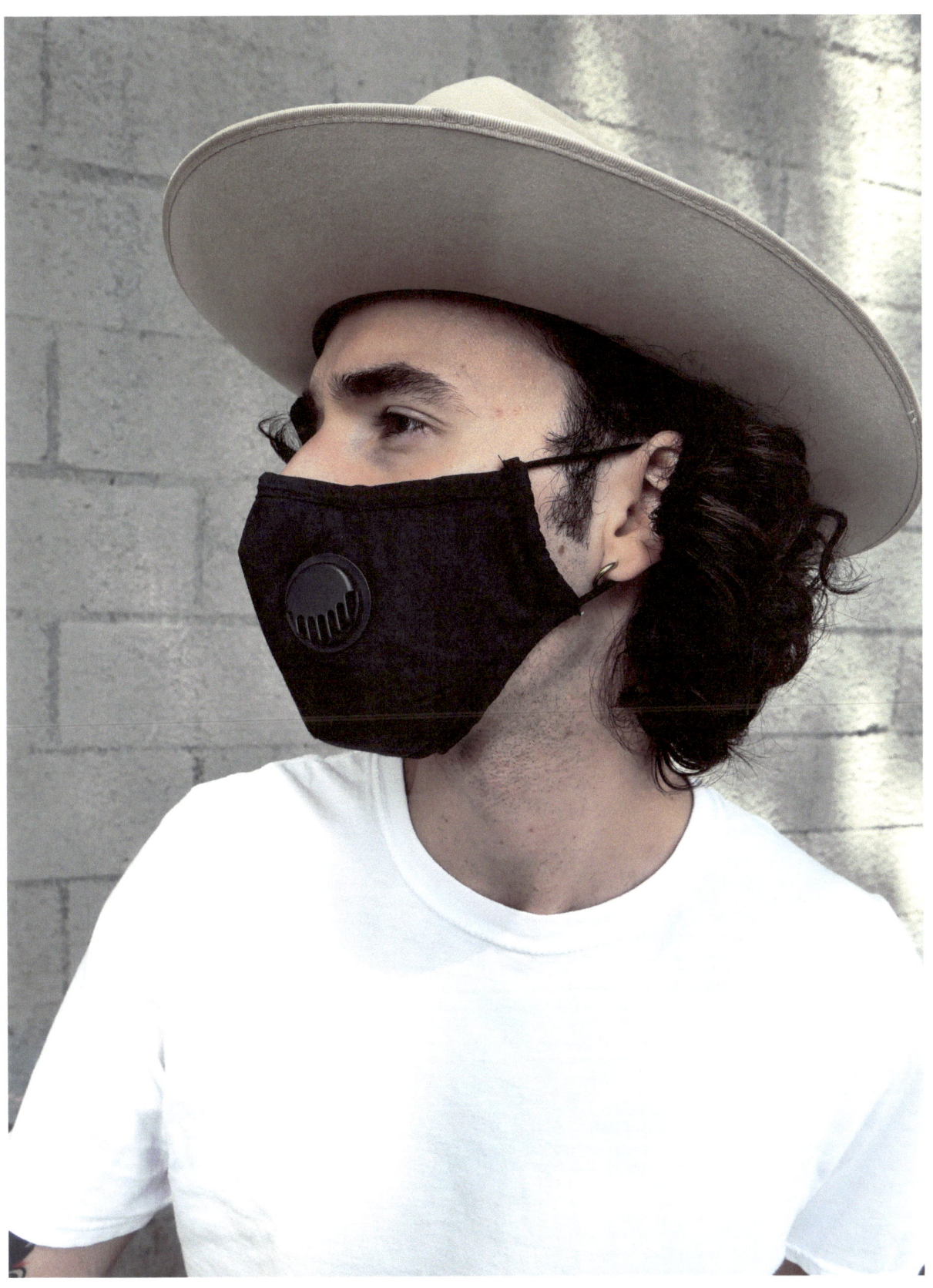

Harry Gamboa Jr.
Striking Distance #7

16 inches x 20 inches
FujiFlex Lightjet Print
Edition of three

Performer: Daniel Carbone-Escamilla

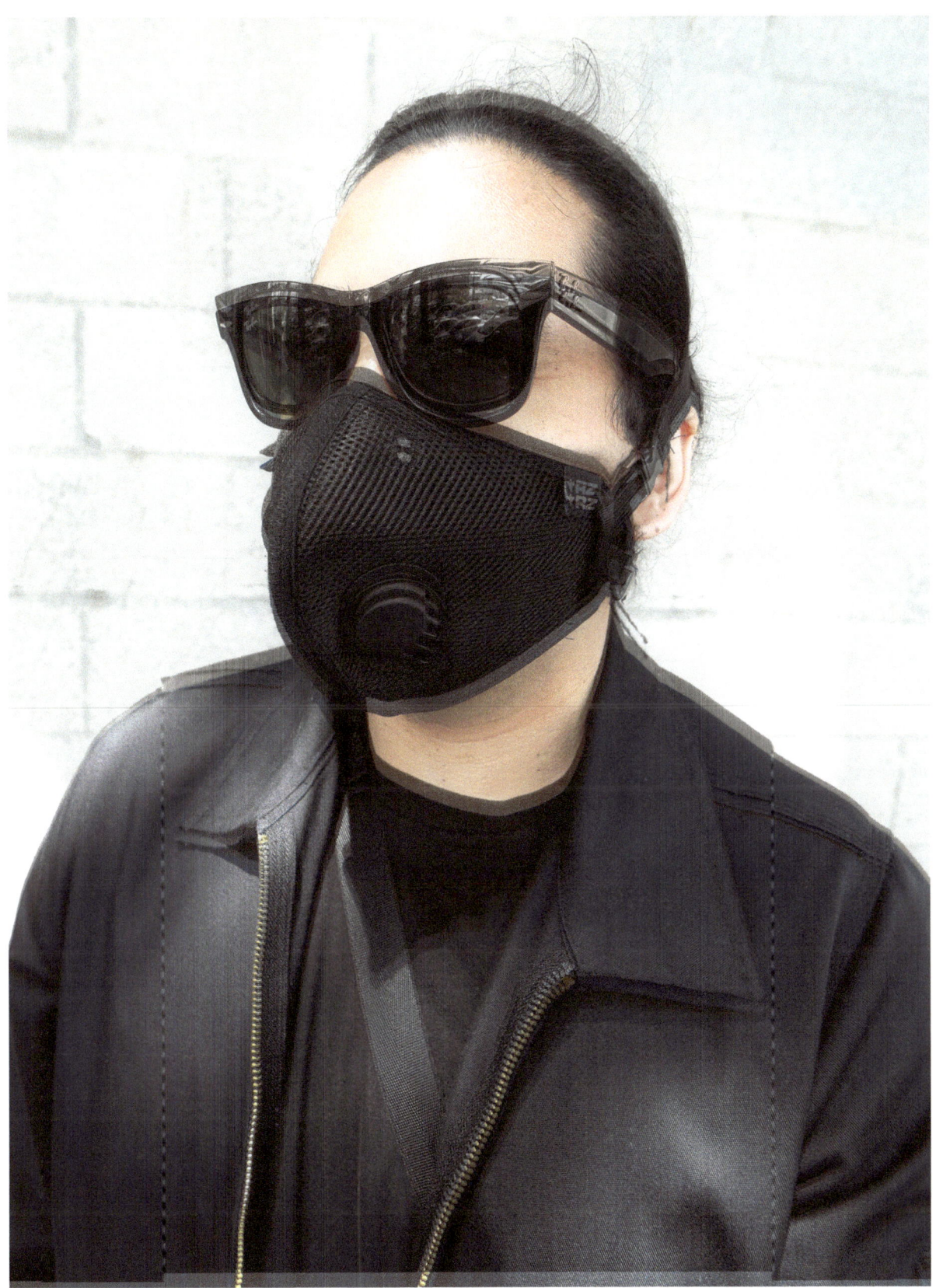

Harry Gamboa Jr.
Striking Distance #8

16 inches x 20 inches
FujiFlex Lightjet Print
Edition of three

Performer: Anais Franco

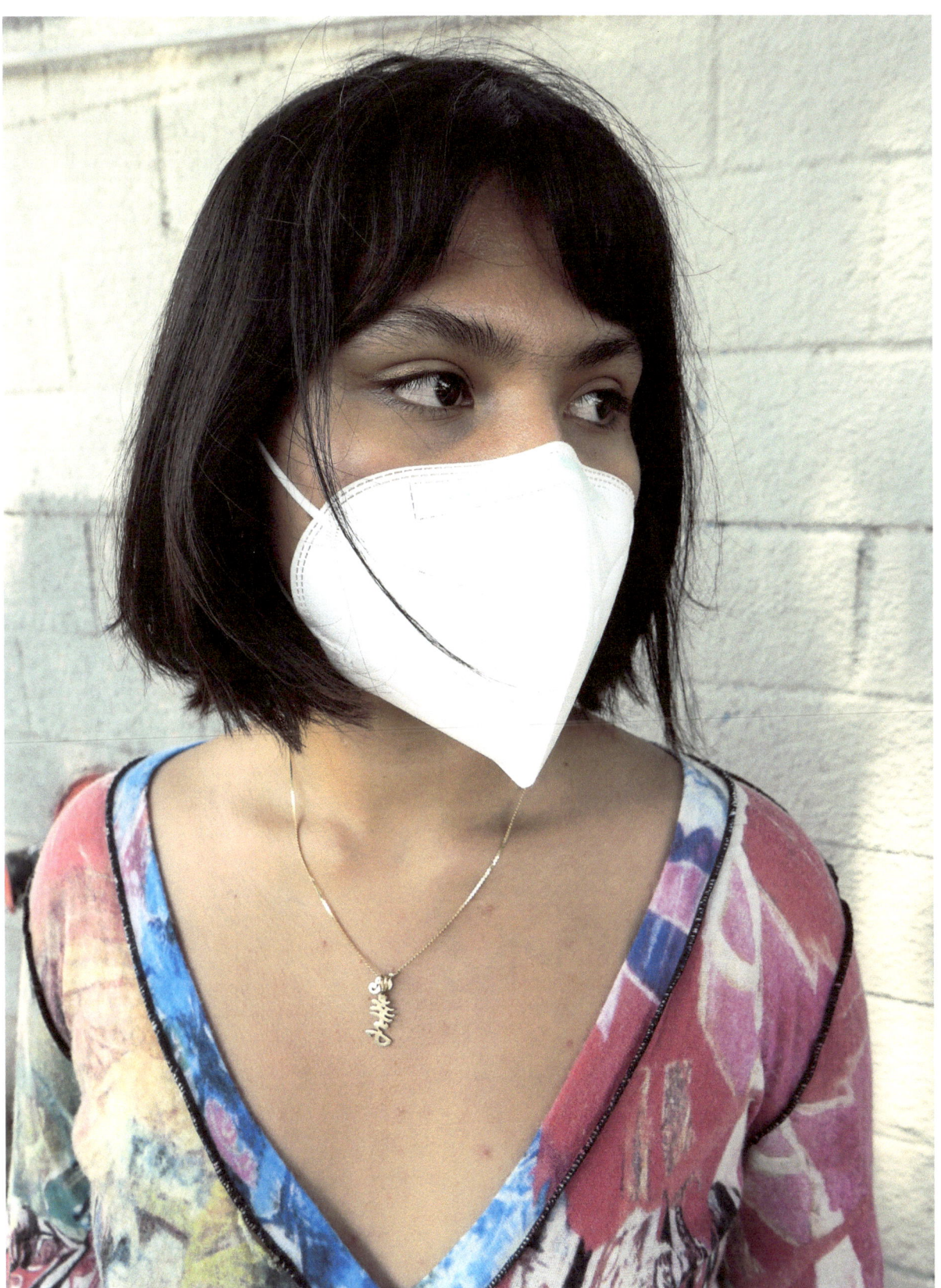

Harry Gamboa Jr.
Striking Distance #9

16 inches x 20 inches
FujiFlex Lightjet Print
Edition of three

Performer: Xavier Cázares Cortéz

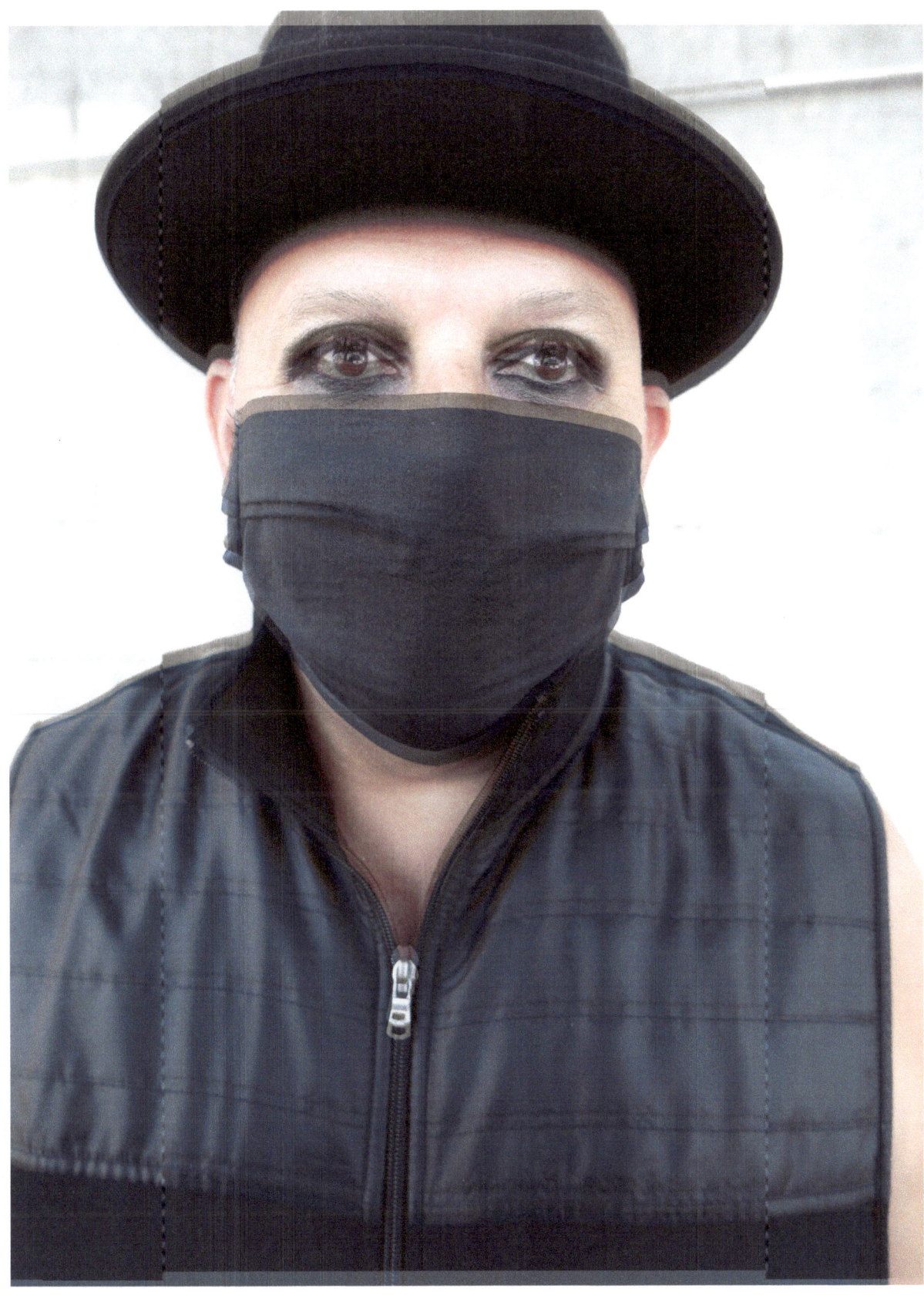

Harry Gamboa Jr.
Striking Distance #10

16 inches x 20 inches
FujiFlex Lightjet Print
Edition of three

Performer: Ruth Murillo

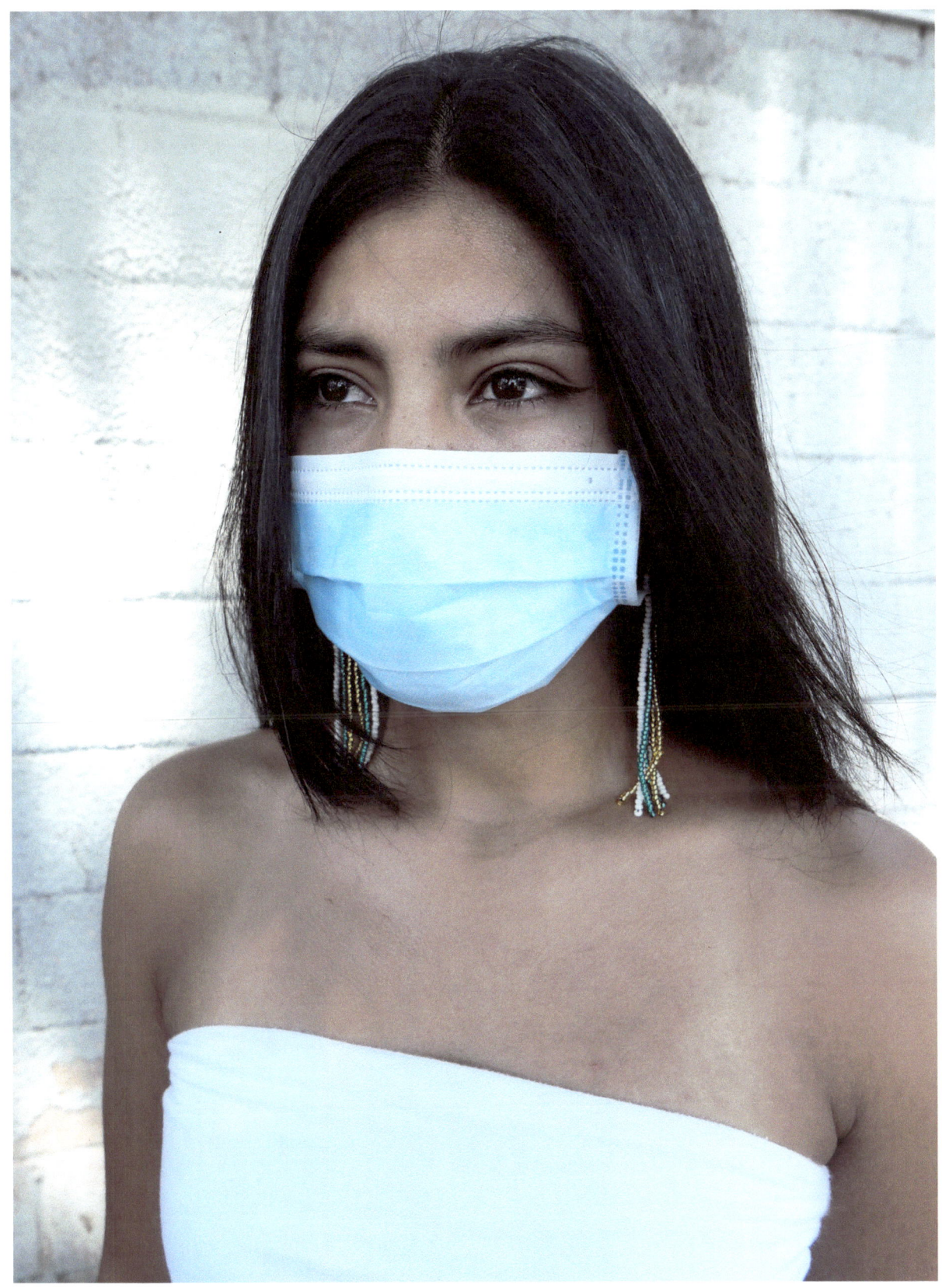

Harry Gamboa Jr.
Striking Distance #11

16 inches x 20 inches
FujiFlex Lightjet Print
Edition of three

Performer: Steven Reyes

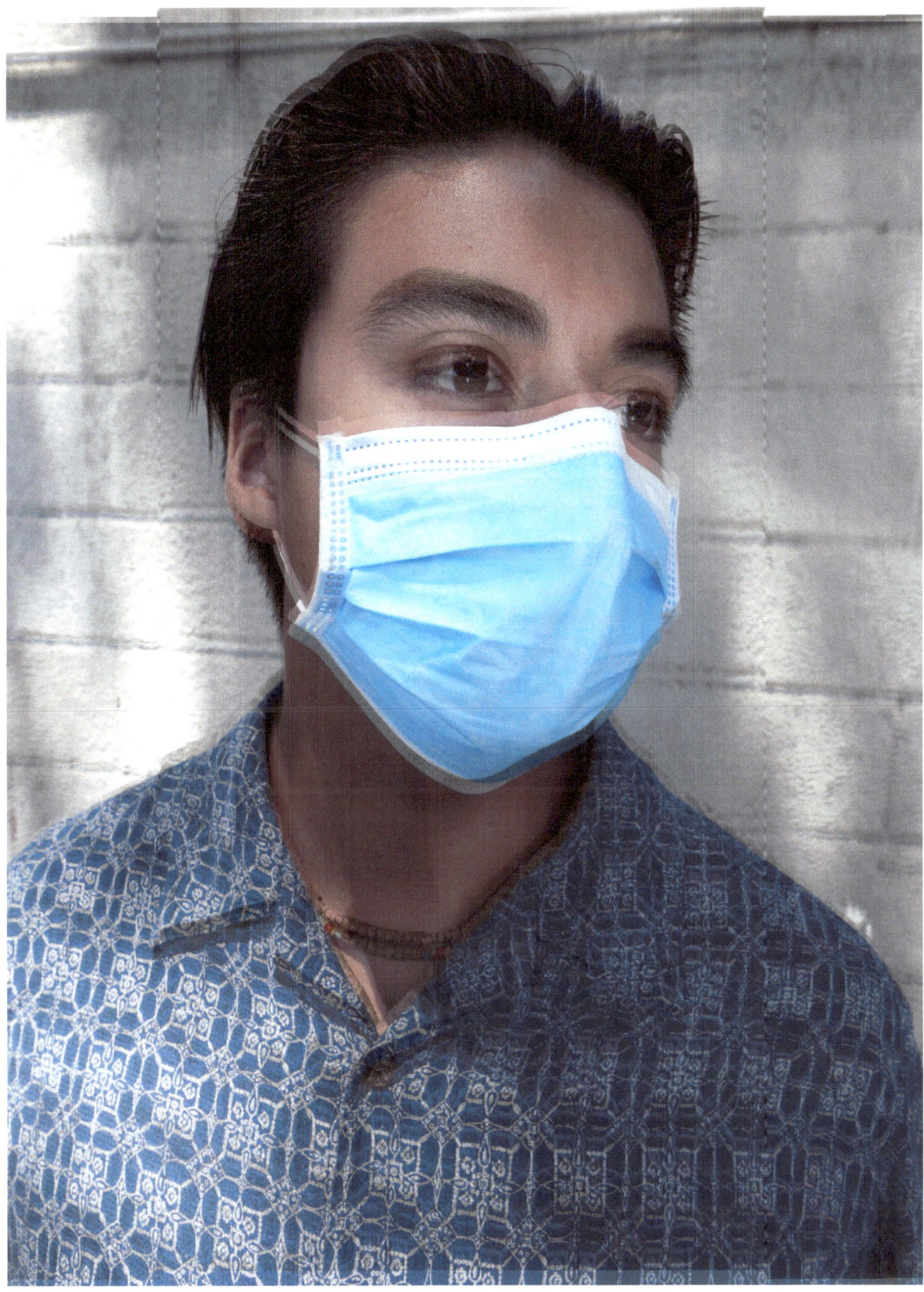

Harry Gamboa Jr.
Striking Distance #12

16 inches x 20 inches
FujiFlex Lightjet Print
Edition of three

Performer: Bayley Mizelle

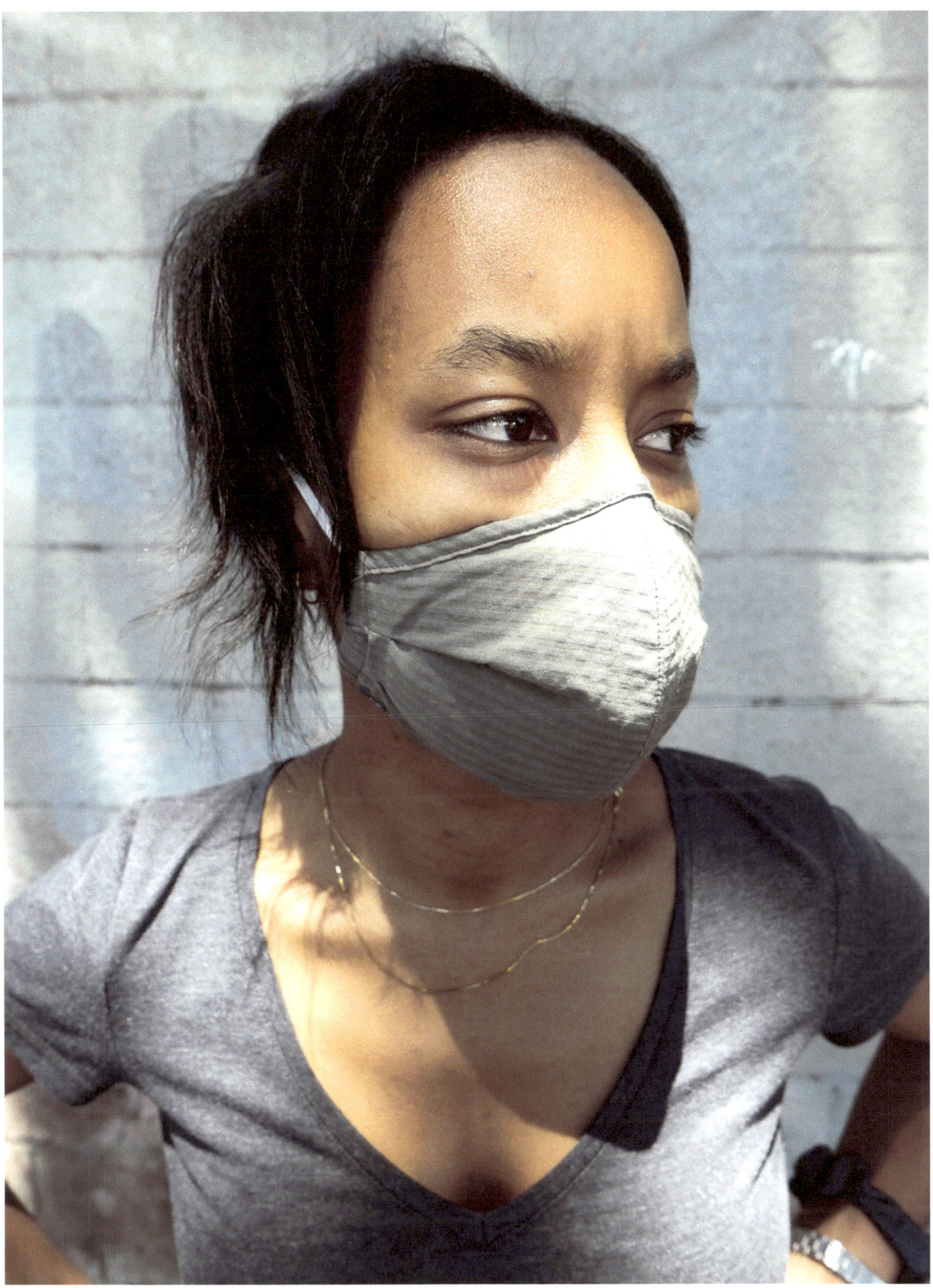

Harry Gamboa Jr.
Striking Distance #13

16 inches x 20 inches
FujiFlex Lightjet Print
Edition of three

Performer: Harper Lyon

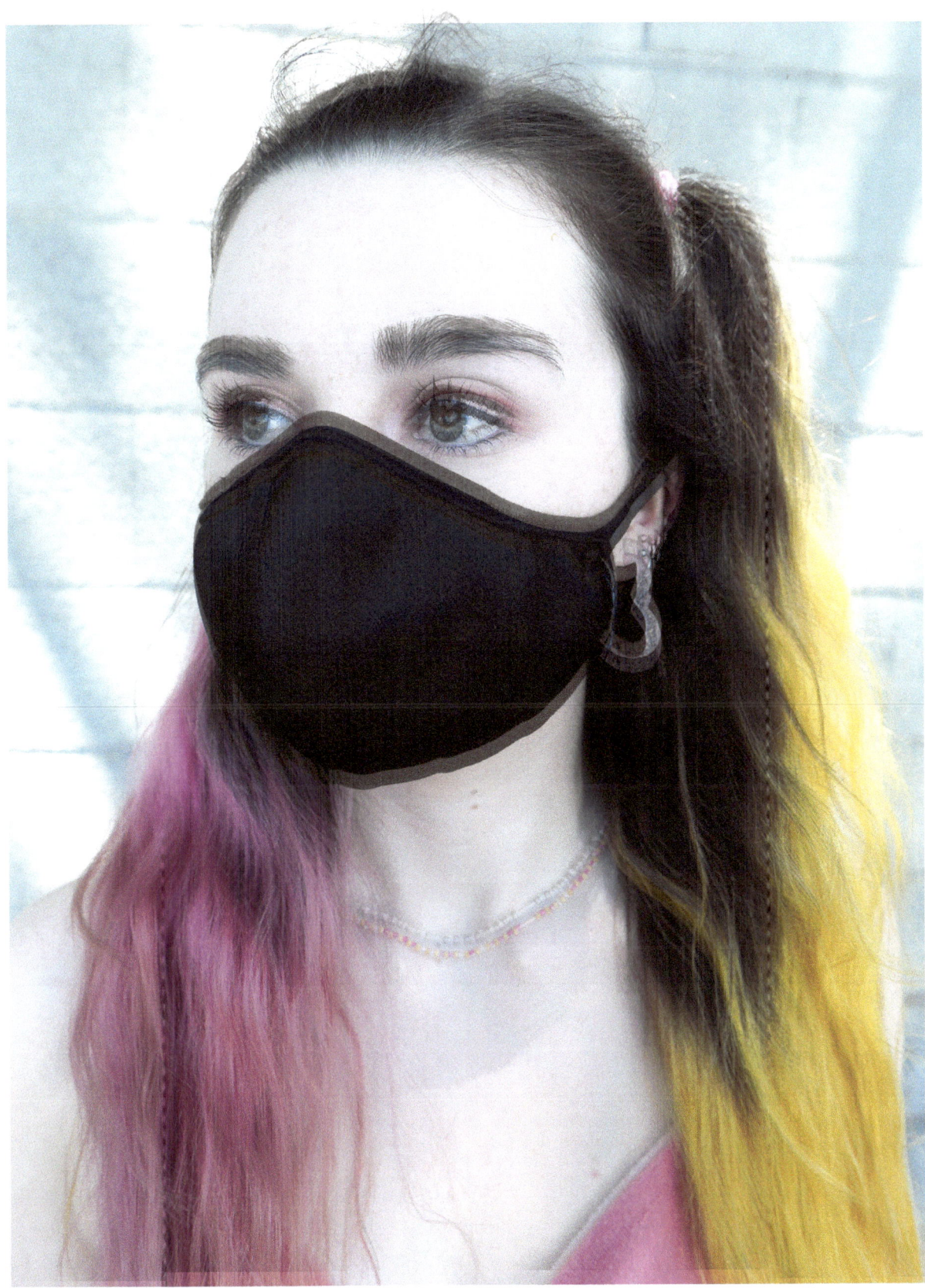

Harry Gamboa Jr.
Striking Distance #14

16 inches x 20 inches
FujiFlex Lightjet Print
Edition of three

Performer: Jaya Inder Kang

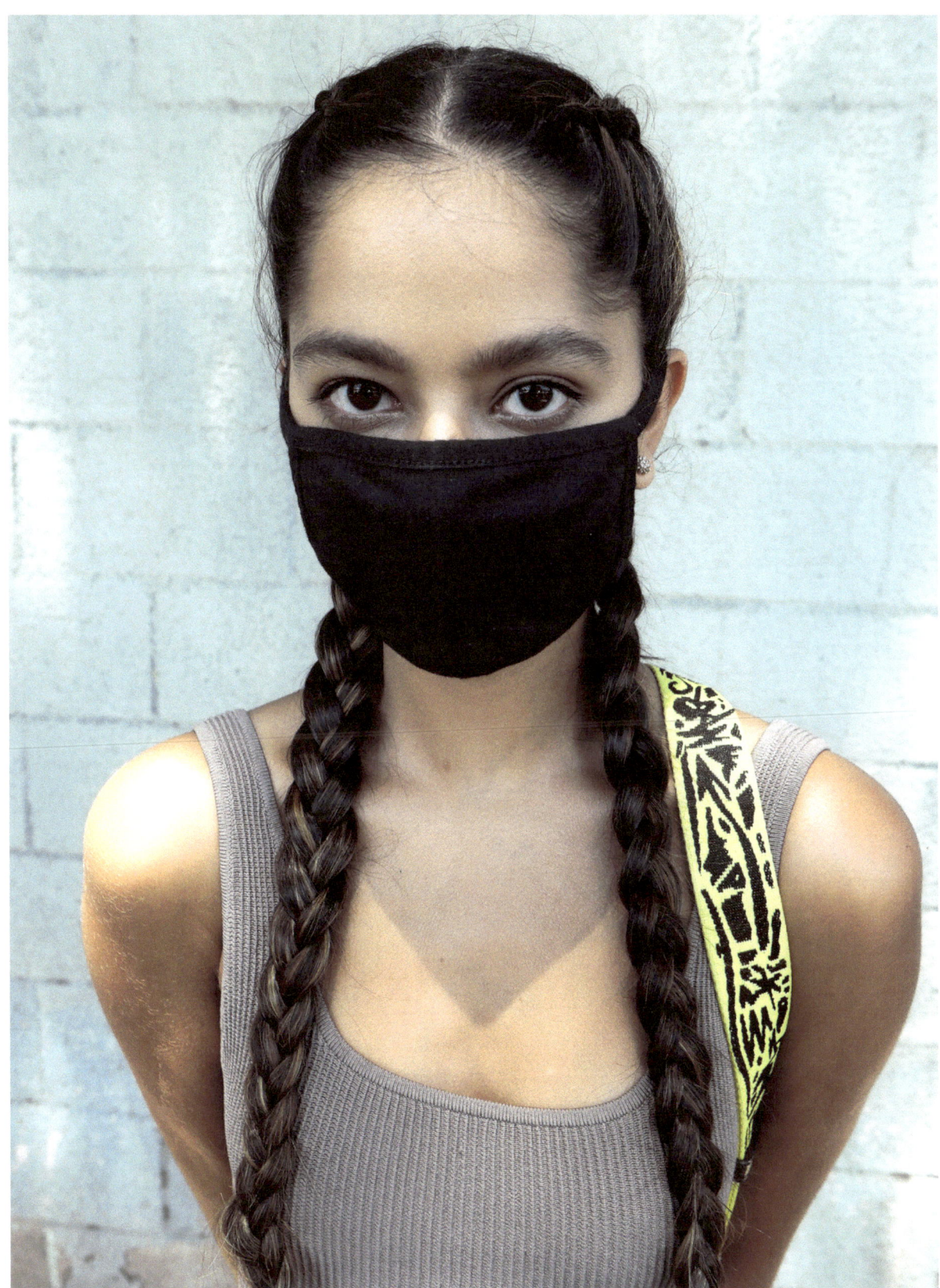

Harry Gamboa Jr.
Striking Distance #15

16 inches x 20 inches
FujiFlex Lightjet Print
Edition of three

Performer: Sydney Mills

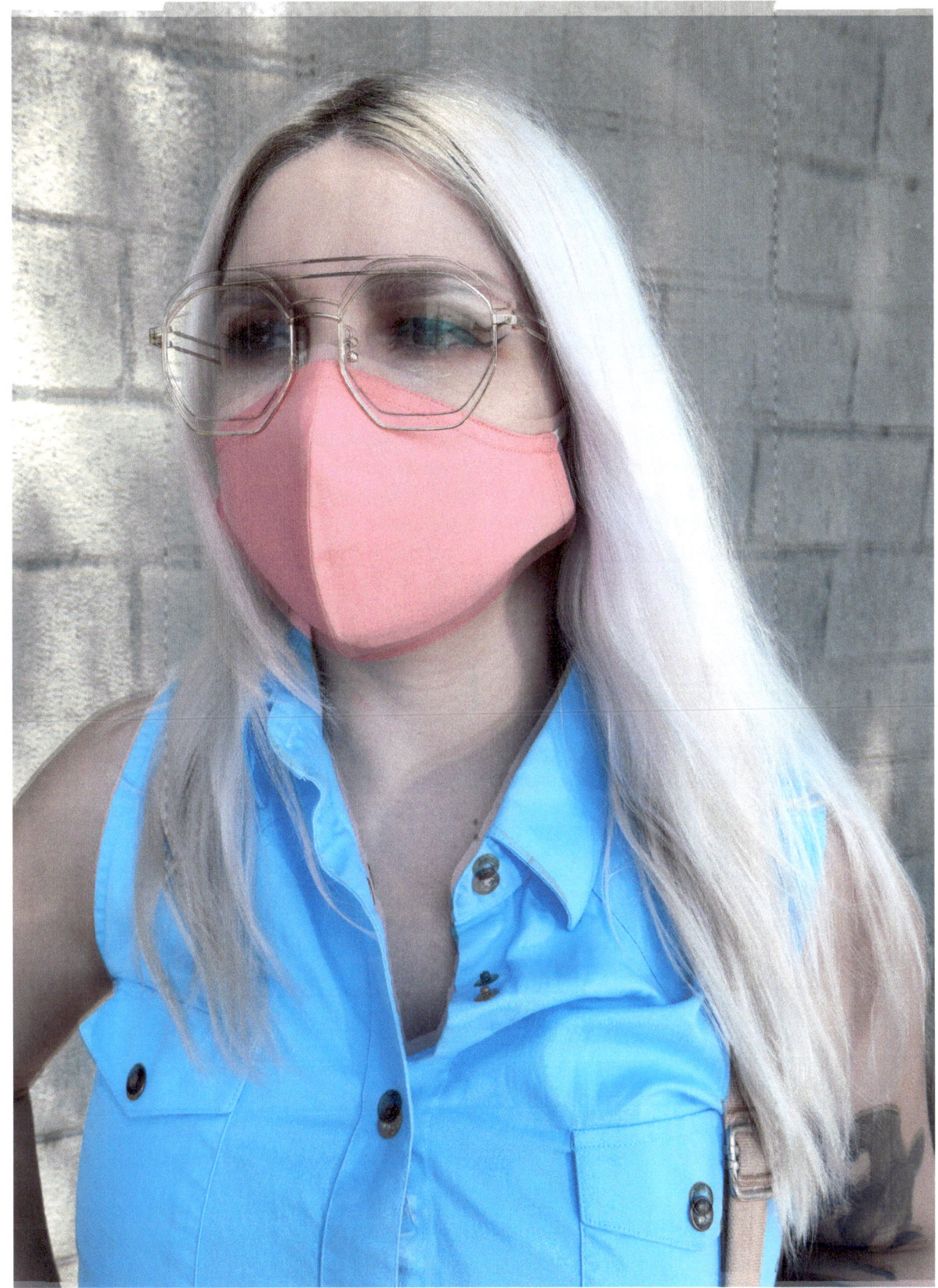

Harry Gamboa Jr.
Striking Distance #16

16 inches x 20 inches
FujiFlex Lightjet Print
Edition of three

Performer: Natalie Hon

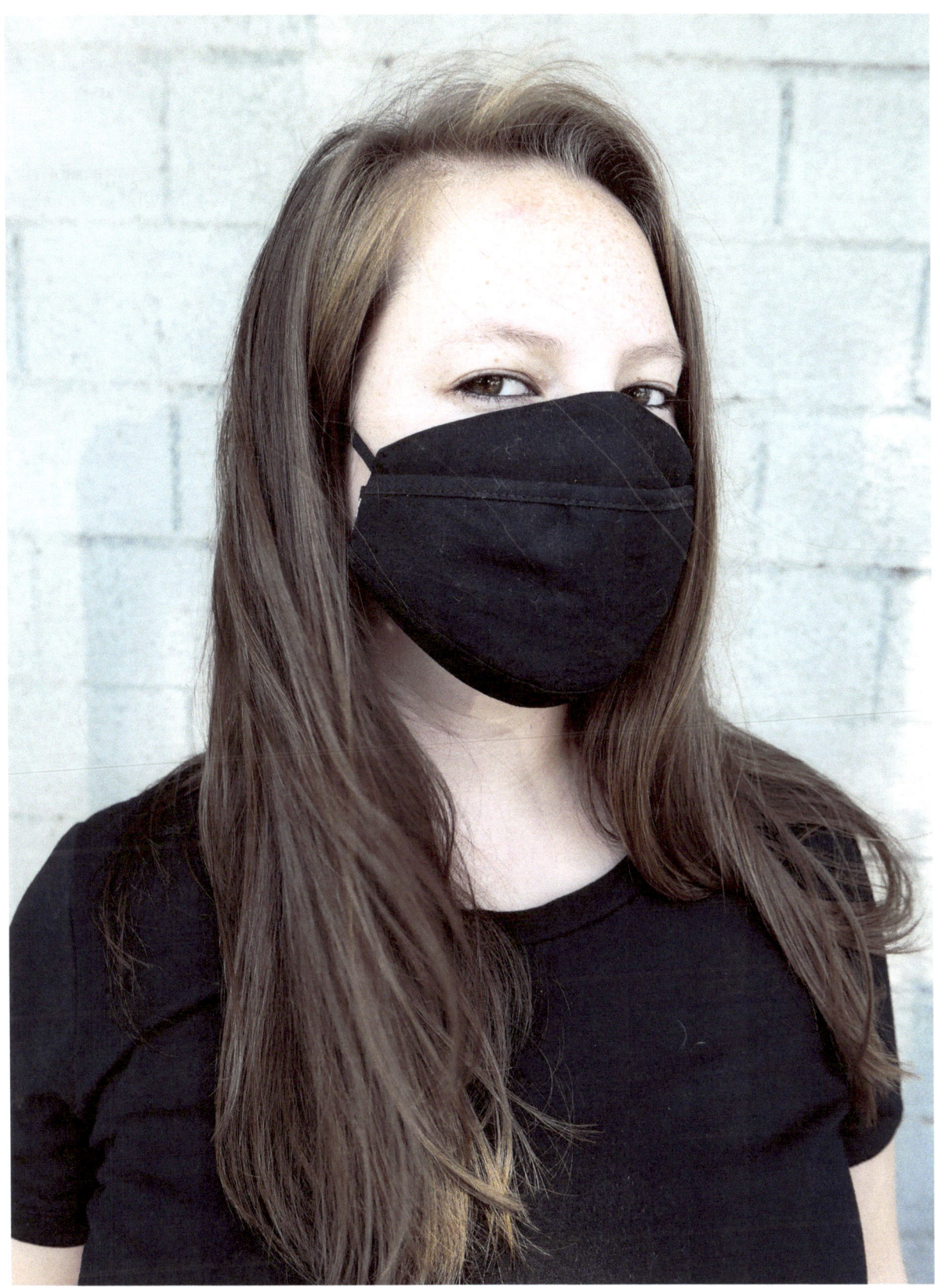

Harry Gamboa Jr.
Striking Distance #17
16 inches x 20 inches
FujiFlex Lightjet Print
Edition of three

Performer: Keaton Macon

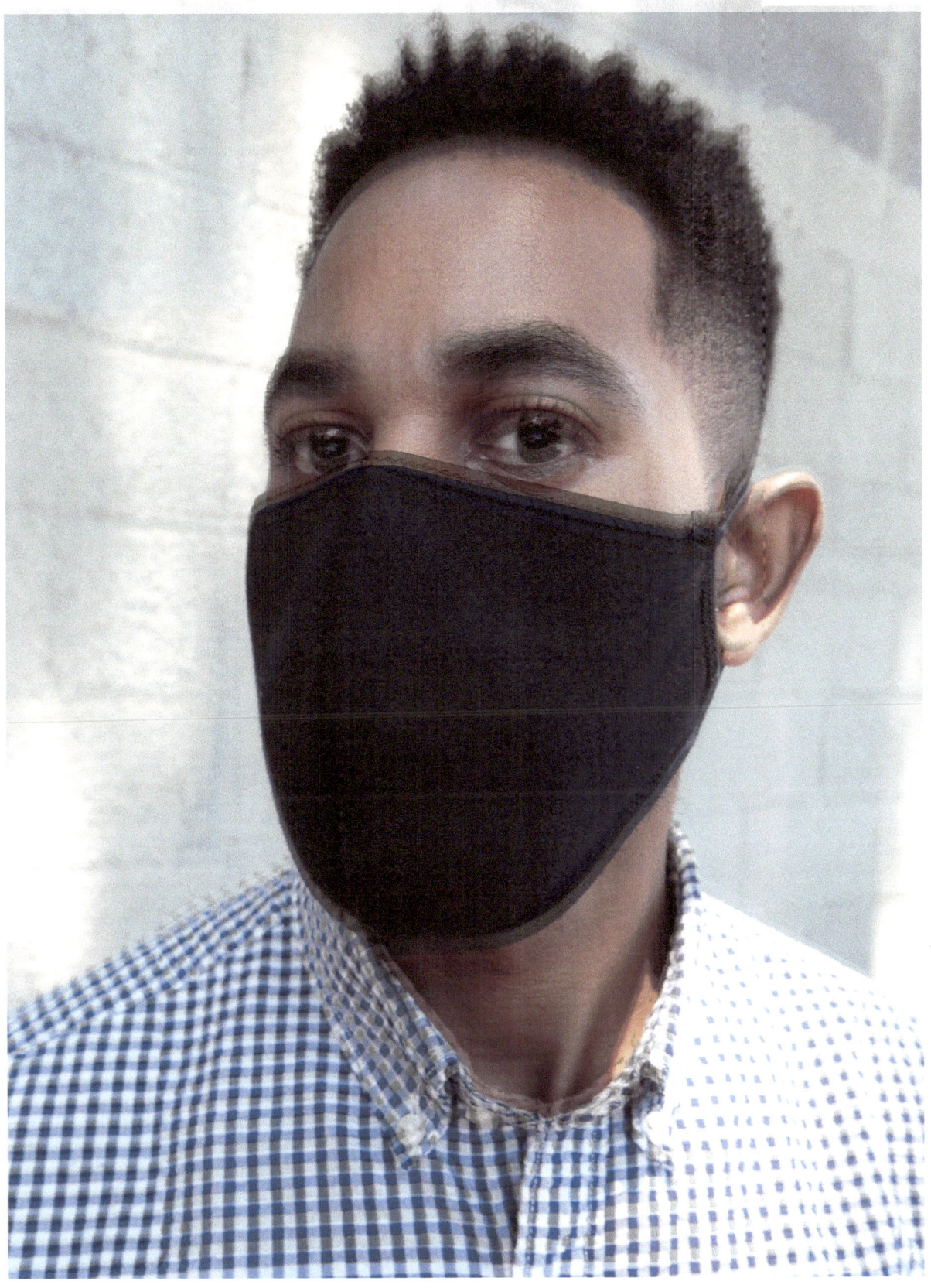

Harry Gamboa Jr.
Striking Distance #18

16 inches x 20 inches
FujiFlex Lightjet Print
Edition of three

Performer: Daniel Centofanti

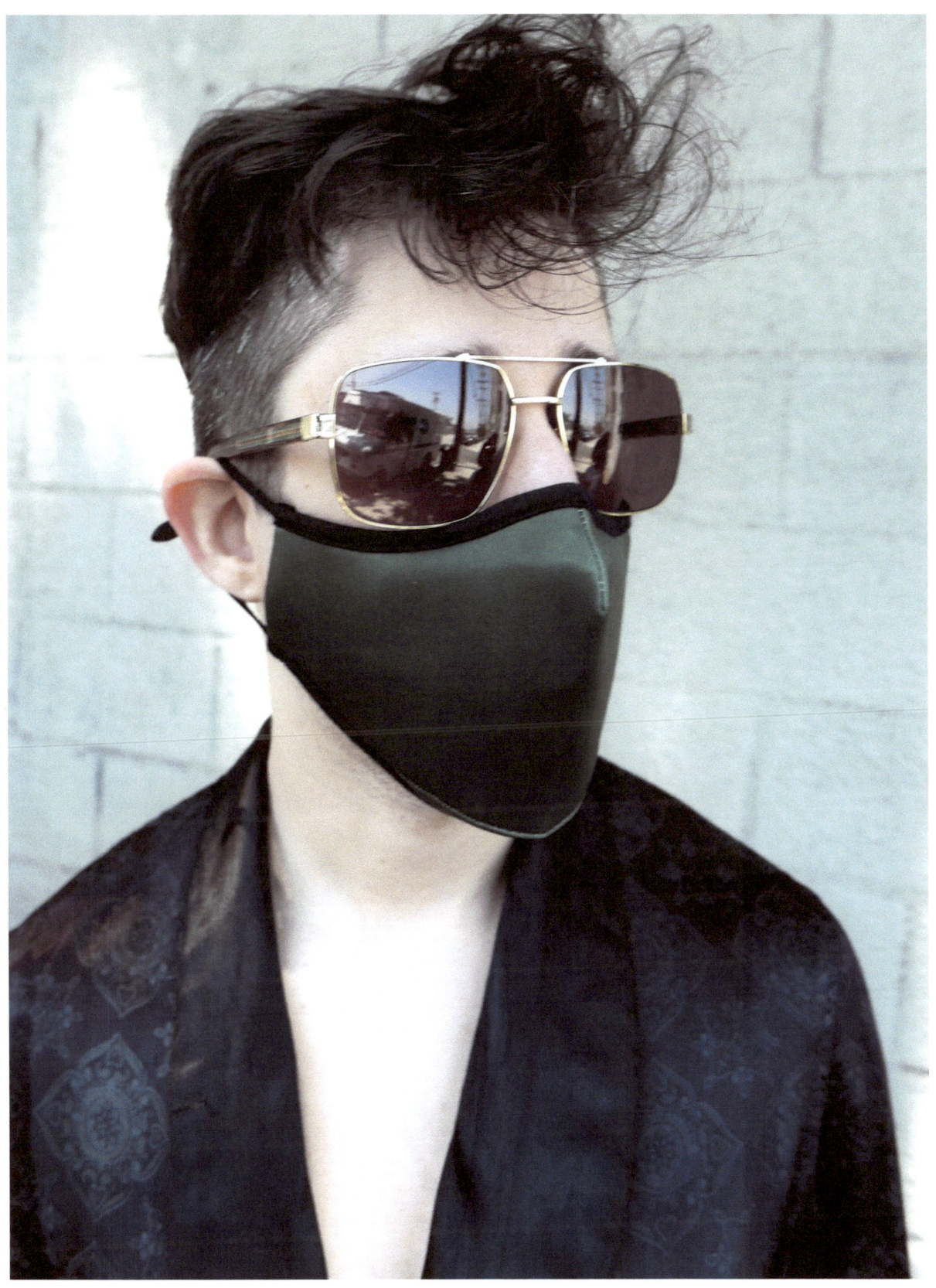

Harry Gamboa Jr.
Striking Distance #19
16 inches x 20 inches
FujiFlex Lightjet Print
Edition of three

Performer: Brenda Reyes-Chavez

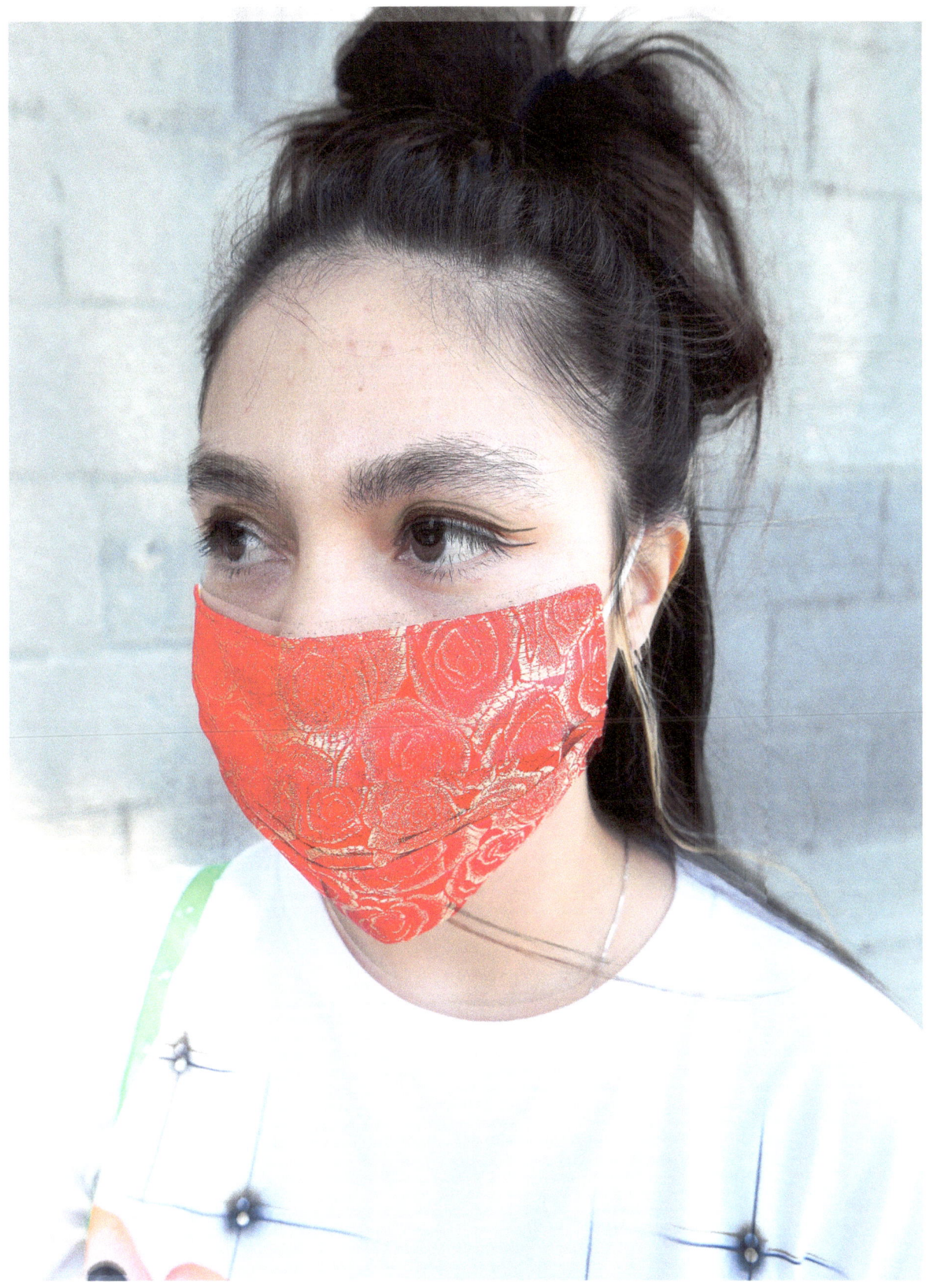

Harry Gamboa Jr.
Striking Distance #1
©2020, Harry Gamboa Jr.
16 inches x 20 inches
FujiFlex Lightjet Print
Edition of three
Performer:
Suné Woods

Harry Gamboa Jr.
Striking Distance #2
©2020, Harry Gamboa Jr.
16 inches x 20 inches
FujiFlex Lightjet Print
Edition of three
Performer:
Benjamin Quiñones

Harry Gamboa Jr.
Striking Distance #3
©2020, Harry Gamboa Jr.
16 inches x 20 inches
FujiFlex Lightjet Print
Edition of three
Performer:
Francesco X. Siqueiros

Harry Gamboa Jr.
Striking Distance #4
©2020, Harry Gamboa Jr.
16 inches x 20 inches
FujiFlex Lightjet Print
Edition of three
Performer:
Calvin Lee

Harry Gamboa Jr.
Striking Distance #5
©2020, Harry Gamboa Jr.
16 inches x 20 inches
FujiFlex Lightjet Print
Edition of three
Performer:
Jazmin Urrea

Harry Gamboa Jr.
Striking Distance #6
©2020, Harry Gamboa Jr.
16 inches x 20 inches
FujiFlex Lightjet Print
Edition of three
Performer:
Henry Williams

Harry Gamboa Jr.
Striking Distance #7
©2020, Harry Gamboa Jr.
16 inches x 20 inches
FujiFlex Lightjet Print
Edition of three
Performer:
Daniel Carbone-Escamilla

Harry Gamboa Jr.
Striking Distance #8
©2020, Harry Gamboa Jr.
16 inches x 20 inches
FujiFlex Lightjet Print
Edition of three
Performer:
Anais Franco

Harry Gamboa Jr.
Striking Distance #9
©2020, Harry Gamboa Jr.
16 inches x 20 inches
FujiFlex Lightjet Print
Edition of three
Performer:
Xavier Cázares Cortéz

Harry Gamboa Jr.
Striking Distance #10
©2020, Harry Gamboa Jr.
16 inches x 20 inches
FujiFlex Lightjet Print
Edition of three
Performer:
Ruth Murillo

Harry Gamboa Jr.
Striking Distance #11
©2020, Harry Gamboa Jr.
16 inches x 20 inches
FujiFlex Lightjet Print
Edition of three
Performer:
Steven Reyes

Harry Gamboa Jr.
Striking Distance #12
©2020, Harry Gamboa Jr.
16 inches x 20 inches
FujiFlex Lightjet Print
Edition of three
Performer:
Bayley Mizelle

Harry Gamboa Jr.
Striking Distance #13
©2020, Harry Gamboa Jr.
16 inches x 20 inches
FujiFlex Lightjet Print
Edition of three
Performer:
Harper Lyon

Harry Gamboa Jr.
Striking Distance #14
©2020, Harry Gamboa Jr.
16 inches x 20 inches
FujiFlex Lightjet Print
Edition of three
Performer:
Jaya Inder Kang

Harry Gamboa Jr.
Striking Distance #15
©2020, Harry Gamboa Jr.
16 inches x 20 inches
FujiFlex Lightjet Print
Edition of three
Performer:
Sydney Mills

Harry Gamboa Jr.
Striking Distance #16
©2020, Harry Gamboa Jr.
16 inches x 20 inches
FujiFlex Lightjet Print
Edition of three
Performer:
Natalie Hon

Harry Gamboa Jr.
Striking Distance #17
©2020, Harry Gamboa Jr.
16 inches x 20 inches
FujiFlex Lightjet Print
Edition of three
Performer:
Keaton Macon

Harry Gamboa Jr.
Striking Distance #18
©2020, Harry Gamboa Jr.
16 inches x 20 inches
FujiFlex Lightjet Print
Edition of three
Performer:
Daniel Centofanti

Harry Gamboa Jr.
Striking Distance #19
©2020, Harry Gamboa Jr.
16 inches x 20 inches
FujiFlex Lightjet Print
Edition of three
Performer:
Brenda Reyes-Chavez

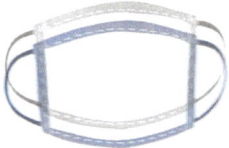

Harry Gamboa Jr. is an artist, writer, and educator.

He is Co-Director of the Photo/Media Program at California Institute of the Arts.

He is the founder and director of Virtual Vérité (2005-2017), the international performance troupe.

He is a co-founder of Asco (1972-1985), the Los Angeles-based performance group.

His work has been exhibited/collected nationally/internationally:

Museum Ludwig, Cologne (2020); Smithsonian National Portrait Gallery, Washington D.C. (2019); Autry Museum of the American West (2018); Marlborough Contemporary, New York (2017); Whitney Museum of American Art, New York (2016, 2015 and 1995 Biennial); Princeton University Art Museum (2015); Centre d'Arts Plastiques Contemporain Bordeaux, France (2014); De Appel, Amsterdam (2014); Triangle France, Marseille, France (2014); Lentos Kunstmuseum Linz, Linz, Austria (2013); Nottingham Contemporary, Nottingham, England (2013); Smithsonian American Art Museum, Washington D.C. (2013); Le Musée d'Art Contemporain, Marseille, France (2013, 2012); Museo Universitario Arte Contemporáneo (UNAM), Mexico City (2013); Tate Liverpool, Liverpool, England (2013); Williams College Museum of Art (2012); Museo del Palacio de Bellas Artes, Mexico City (2011, 1981); Museum of Contemporary Art, Los Angeles (2011, 2010); Musée de l'Élysée, Lausanne, Switzerland (2009); Los Angeles County Museum of Art (2011, 2008, 2001); Centre Pompidou, Paris, France (2006); Statens Museum for Kunst, Copenhagen, Denmark (1996); (1994); Museo de Arte Moderno, Mexico City (1978); Museo Alvar y Carmen T. Carrillo Gil, Mexico City (1978):

Books and eBooks

by

Harry Gamboa Jr.

https://www.amazon.com/author/harrygamboajr

www.ingramcontent.com/pod-product-compliance
Lightning Source LLC
Chambersburg PA
CBHW051926210526
45473CB00006B/2155